Poison Begets Poison

Owen Hill

SPUYTEN DUYVIL

New York City

Deepest thanks to Noah Ross for his friendship and encouragement as these poems progressed.

Thanks also to Joseph Lease, early reader of the completed book. Our ongoing conversation on poetry (and everything) is the basis for a lifelong friendship.

Some of these poems (in earlier versions) appeared in *Baest* and *Brooklyn Rail*. Thanks to Noah and to Anselm Berrigan.

Cover drawing: *weary complications* by Liz Leger (© 2024)
Cover art photography : Nan Davenport

Library of Congress Control Number: 2025934098

City Dwellers/After Brecht

Cover Your Tracks

Tearful goodby airline parking lot
Don't come back
Cover your tracks
If you bump into another
From times past
Pass like a stranger without a look

Pull down the hat don't show face
Whatever you do

Do nothing twice don't repeat
Otherwise your story won't seem
Plausible or fresh

Your only project is to submerge
Don't stop along the way

There are no signs worth heeding

The Cities are Made for You

Since the cities are large
Complicated to navigate
Directions are there for you
Who haven't learned the rules

Joyfully we await your arrival
Doors unlocked tables set
Be open to suggestions
We are too

You needn't be sure of intentions
We consider all suggestions
Answer questions as they arise

Everything actually was planned
Before your arrival

You who haven't caught onto the grift

THE STREET

You've tasted the gas looked down the
Barrel you've had due process we'll have
The report You have been shot don't get up
Too quickly
You have been shot don't turn
Around
Things got jumbled wait until
The smoke clears
Stay down

Here it Comes

Reality will come to you in dry and factual terms
Undeniable and beyond communication it
Won't recognize you or your weary complications

CHRONOS

The cities may change but you may not
The rubble's kept low to prop up the stones
We may kill you though we don't need to
Might be best to stay inside

You may change but the cities may not
The stones don't flatten to rubble at least
Not that you'll notice we didn't care enough
To kill you the times just moved things along

SOMETHING'S WRONG

You fear that you can no longer make a living
Nobody needs the stuff you make the person you are
You have been moved out someone else lives here

Strange how the world breathes on its own
Somewhat dangerous below but not by design
You are pursued but don't respect your pursuers

It is and it isn't the natural order of things
Maybe you fall into a river some reach the banks
Others drift to the sea you struggle rivers are indifferent

This particular situation doesn't involve trust faith or reason
The distrust between classes is another matter

Fifth Wheel

Towers of tires by the side of the highway
Sometimes inexplicably one will catch fire
Ignoring the others it's another toxic day

We enter your head when it starts to ache
You rub your temples
Realize you are a fifth wheel

We're in your head and on your shoulders
From here to the horizon as you search
For a word that allows you an exit

Without making too much of a scene
Finally plainly say please I want out
We answer you will stay until we say so

We' answer plainly too don't think
We're villains just keeping you informed transparency is our stock in trade

Don't admit the the world's gone toxic
Don't go for your gun have a glass of water
The world isn't really that bad we just have no space For you

How it Flies and How it Rolls

When years ago I attempted a minor insurrection
And tried to study labor's relation to profit I suddenly
Understood how everything is managed and manipulated

And at the same time I did not understand so turned
Away semi-ignorant but somehow knowing
That I could get myself into some deeper shit

When it occurred that achievement invention discovery
Could be used for greater misery rage
And lamentation followed but I turned away

The thought that what they did and how
Was intolerable shocked me but mostly Frightened me
That those that live by doing damage to others

A situation upheld only by crimes committed
So effortlessly would just as easily damage me

Heavy gunfire from beyond the bay
Militia in full kit
Couple down by the beach
Under a blanket
Second hand military trucks
Glide on down all along the
Coast history written/cheap style
Of novelettes nobody reads

We built on rock we built on sand

The rock caved in the sand muddied

The generals go straight

From HQ to lunatic asylums

The possessions of the haves

Grow

Protest you will be beaten

Don't protest and you will be beaten

Too

Fog covers the Bridge's
Neatly discreet parts

Headlights come on
Like little medals

Across the pockets
Of lapels

Scrim covered they
Nearly shine on

The military hand-
me-down cop cars

Police break pride with heavy hands
You'll get no glimpse of heaven from down here
You don't always land on your feet but who does

THE DISCREET CHARM

They ate all the birds in the trees
We ate all the birds in the trees

Now cursing fate
When lunch is late

HOMILY

From the new transmitters come the same old idiocies
Same meat on old forks finds new appetites

Yet on the outskirts the trees spread fine branches
Protecting the abuser and the hero all the same

Beatings begin and beatings end

Homily 2

The guests have full plates yet they handed you
An empty plate and cup you ask
When will I be served they say later

Outside the useless moon half hides
Behind glass buildings you notice

And appreciate as best you can you see
The gods of revolt knee deep
In a bog

Wading toward you but not very fast

PLUMBING

Under the cities the sewers
Inside and under you don't want to know
Inside your insides don't even consider

Nobody praises those rivers
Everybody loves the ocean

Yet everything drains to the ocean

When/When?

The houses of the wealthy finally collapse
The help the employees will go under
Stay away from the houses of the rich

The whales and the sharks devour
Small fish are lost in the blood circles
Stay away from sharks and whales

The rich go their way like the gods
Their wake will be uncontrollable
Stay away from gods

One Last Grievance

A third of the city sleeps through graveyard shift
Another slow night but the screams of the marked can be heard
Much louder to those without windows or doors

What happens to the holes when the cheese is
Gone when the choice is death or an inadequate life
When the things that you said tore the heart

When you understand everything and run out of stories
Say it like it should be said/every heart torn to shreds

COLLATERAL DAMAGE

what besides the multicultural population
drew you to buy in the East Bay Hills

being a dad teaches you to better explain
things to employees eventually they

jump up and say look look I see it too

everyone becomes very engaged

as an owner of a gallery that represents
over twenty artists many from abroad

I can really embrace the community

the work/life balance allows for time at play

or get fired you'll feel better

do the good work of selling
here at the new commons
you are the new commoners

a life raft or a lifeboat or a safety net
a buffer or a bufferin a parachute
a really able enabler an air hose
a crate shovel

just a park swing made of fur
generalities that glitter

appealing words will sell the product
even before inspection or
before the product is conceived

appealing to backers and suckers alike
suckers lemmings backers
let the sheep be sheared

even when the body falls from the doorway
even after the windows are lit with gunfire
even after the latest bait and switch
none of the marks get paid in full

everyone will become very engaged
appealing words will sell the product
like happy jewels avoiding the dark

bait and switch the payoff
golden smatterings in the bushes
ectoplasm hovers like northern lights

to be seized then swept
clean brain dead and
Shanghai'd following the
flashing light that plays
around His hem

they flee knee deep in tule fog
abstracts the fooling and sliding thus
as through quicksand they cry
they are the suckers

doing the good work of selling things I fly above the wind
when the fix is in your kind is not your kind
the fools are never paid in full what they get is what you decide

I fly above the wind yet can't rise above
air like gravel sand like oil
a desire to soar a desire to perish
creating clouds of disdain

silver lucifer
at the chemistry set
upsets the laboratory
of language

they flee from me but
I don't miss 'em

lemmings at the barbeque swiftly falling
into the light blinded and groping
through a veil or an avalanche

events vague and complex share a smile
with the body pile

we might have given birth to a butterfly
but were slaves to mental lethargy
finding joy in the hideous

blink hard before you know it
you are up against it

what besides the bohemian legacy and breezy views
brought you to these East Bay Hills
what besides security and a multi-
cultural environment

you won't believe the restaurant scene
and all through town the fucking posts
above street level there we seek relief

the rude roaring hector of the streets
through double glass windows rumbling
sweet grunting from the fucking posts

gastro gyms raw bars
Acme bread Tokyo fish
scandals at the posts
you will not believe
the restaurant scene

Westbrae Gilman Rockridge
Temescal the East Bay Hills
we can claim loss of use
when we have no use for
you

CBA

Believe in creating and sustaining an equitable workplace
Unless the committee's vote is less than unanimous
Based on and agreed upon process all workers are
Members and required to use personal vehicles as parties
Agree Company must periodically supply all
As needed until the differences are washed away
And the heartbreak is admitted to be contained in heaven's
Water beyond argument flowing away from mountains as defined here

As defined here not otherwise defined
As a grievance   or as the naked eye
Or as a pacing above on deck until excused to move away
Or that in the event of resignation may swim in water
The color green as in any disagreement or dispute
Must hard cut through fog's density or otherwise
Bear the weight of the cost of arbitration without sharing
Direct control of the operation

The direct control of the operation as equal and fair
To name it directly separate from musky chromosomes
Separate from the eerie sea   for purposes of bereavement
Or otherwise capped form accrual neither approved
Nor rejected nor recognized by designated
directors managers supervisors   rehires or
consultants comma comma period

Periods of several hours in succession overtime notwithstanding
The parties agree to a complete nothing
                              therefore warfare
The directors shall have their prior articles herein wreckballed
Until at night one drop of rain closes it all and parties agree
They want this night to end

At completion of malicious intent all have the right to be free
As defined delineated   in good faith attempted
To swim in green rivulets in the night when shifts have closed
Theirs in the spirit of full disclosure glide noiselessly
Among bigger ships with express right to sink all
Ships too large until the skies leak bands of
Light and smokes soar into themselves creating new
poisons that oblitarate the poisons of the past

OWEN HILL is a novelist and poet. *The Giveaway: The Clay Blackburn Story*, forthcoming in the spring from PM Press, an omnibus of his crime fiction, includes three novels and a short story. He has reviewed crime novels for the Los Angeles Times and the East Bay Express. In 2005 he was awarded the Howard Moss residency at Yaddo. He is co-editor (with Jerry Thompson) of *Berkeley Noir* for Akashic Press. A memoir, *Hands on a Mirror,* is available from Bootstrap Press. Owen worked for many years in a second-hand bookstore in Berkeley. He is currently an organizer for the Industrial Workers of the World.